J2 One Wild Ride

By Jim Browne

Names, people, places, and incidents are nonfictional life stories as told by the author. Names of individuals outside of those consenting to their use in this story have been changed for privacy unless otherwise stated.

Copyright © 2024 by Jim Browne
No part of this book may be reproduced or used in any manner without written permission of the Copyright owner except for use of quotations in a book review.

First paperback edition November 2024

Book design & Editing by Mathew E. Ruley
Cerolian Arts, LLC

Eagle image by https://www.freeimages.com/
Heart Image by juicy_fish on Freepik

ISBN 978-1-7348122-7-5 (Hardback)

Library of Congress Control Number: 2024920827

First Edition

Delton, Michigan
Cerolian Arts LLC

This book is dedicated to all those booktok girlies that love nothing more than to be left alone with a good book. Those same girls that ended up falling in love with some trucker they met online who would do anything to put a smile on her face. So, grab nachos and an *iceless coke*, we are embarking ***on an adventure***.

CONTENTS
J2
One Wild Ride

The Only Chapter

CHAPTER I   PG. 3

Some Other Stuff

PHOTO GALLERY   PG. 18
ABOUT THE AUTHOR   PG. 40
ACKNOWLEDGMENTS   PG. 42

COOL EAGLE PICTURE
PG. ROMAN NUMERAL ONE
(BEFORE THIS)

Content Warnings

Gross Displays of Affection.

ADHD Randomness.

not good grammer.

Poor, Punctuation!

Overabundance of Love and Happiness.

Lack of Smut.

ONE WILD RIDE
CHAPTER 1, THE ONLY CHAPTER

It's that crazy guy you've gone an entire year with so far. It's been one wild ride for sure. So many ups and some rough downs. But this past year, I have to admit, is the best year I feel I've ever had - because I've got to enjoy you being in it.

When we met, I had no clue what I was looking for or what life had in store for me. So, I jumped on the good ol *FB Dating* and decided to dip my toes back into the dating pool. I'll be honest I had low self-esteem and even lower hope that I'd ever even get a response from anyone. Then I came across this gorgeous woman and read her profile. I remember saying to myself:

"What's the worst that will happen? Get ignored? Fuck it."

So I messaged.

You wouldn't believe what happened! This absolute Goddess of a woman, I mean just absolutely drop dead gorgeous responded!!! *Holy shit balls over here*. Okay, okay, okay, play it *coooooool*. So, we chat for a bit, and I started to feel it. There was something different here. I wasn't about to risk messing this up or losing a chance with her so I got with my boss and said I need to get home. We had set up a date that she was pretty excited for. Admittedly it was like an "Eh but I'll do whatever." Kinda' date for a chance with her.

We continued to chat over the next few days as I worked closer and closer to getting home to meet her. The whole time thinking *imma' screw this up* or *there's no way this is real*. But I didn't. I made it home, jumped on my bike, and headed off to the address I was given. The loudness of my music on that drive to drown out my nerves was deafening. Got closer and closer to the destination so it was time to activate 'calm and collected' mode. *Can't fuck this up*. I'm gross and sweaty at this point but this was it. I pulled into the driveway. Let her know I was there. *Okay Jim. Don't forget to breathe*. You can do this…

Oh my god, and out she came.

This absolutely stunning woman that's had me wanting to message all day and night until this moment. Just ***wow***. She's real. She was wearing this cute black top with, I think, flowers or some kinda' design on it, blue jeans, and just a radiant glow all around her.

We hugged and I stuttered out some words. No clue what was said. Honestly a blur at this moment because I was so captivated by her beauty.

So, what I failed to mention, is she has 2 kids. Fun fact about me, never dated anyone with kids so… Full-blown terror? The answer is **yup**. But that's fine. Not like imma' meet them the first time meeting her so no reason to sweat it. Besides, her daughter doesn't like anyone she dated. So, all I gotta' do is be myself and I can add myself to the list. But seriously. I gotta' try and win over this gorgeous, smart, funny, charismatic, and just so down to earth woman AND *her teenage daughter* who was described as the 'typical teenager with a touch of emo and a love for hating everyone.' Awesome! Easy peasyyyyy.

Fucking kill me, I'm not gonna' win this.

But again. First time meeting her. Don't need to worry about that now. Slow your roll guy.

We had head inside before we could head out, soooooo, I follow her inside. I walk awkwardly into her kitchen and of course start lookin' around. She seemed pretty organized but also had a possible cup addiction. Pretty sure I saw like 10 just from looking around. But hey, cups are cool? Maybe. Oh well, that's her thing.

Anyways where was I?

Oh yeah. So, she's like "Wanna' watch tv?"

I'm like, "Sure."

Whatever keeps me in this AC cause its hot as fuck outside is all I could think. But that sounds good. So, we step into her dining room and **boom**. *Both kids. Right there.*

Stomach pit drop. They were hungry and so her and them were trying to figure out what they wanted. Of course, kids being kids, they wanted all the food. So of course I'm like 'Welp. Go for it. Try and win them over and impress her.' So, I tell them to tell me what they want and ill order it. Of course, she's polite and is all "No that's okay, you don't need to," and all that but of course I insist and start to put in an order for Chinese. They got so much food, lmao. It was like around $80 or $90. She felt terrible but I played it cool. No biggie. Feed them and we can go get some food too. All I could think about was her kids thinking "Who the fuck is this guy and why is he here? Oh well, least he bought food," lol.

Welp, lets go start part one of our date.

~Part One of Our Date~

    She suggested a Mexican place down the street so I was like, "let's do it." She's gluten free and i eat anything that tastes good without knowing what's in it, so letting her pick I felt was the safe bet. Speaking of safe tho, I had to ride shotgun. Ughhhhh. *I hope she don't kill us.* I've rode with some pretty bad drivers. But she didn't. It was a nice calm ride over. Took, I dunno, 10 minutes? Got to the restaurant and I had to check if it was open. Sure didn't seem like it. So, what did I do? Gave a thumbs up that she could come in……

Bro. The fuck you doing? Should'a went out and got her and brought her in.

Ughhhh, fucking this all up.

Stop it. Breathe. Okay. We can overcome that blunder.

Sat down and ordered some drinks while we looked at the menu. She got a coke with no ice. I remember thinking *'who gets drinks without ice? So weird.'* lol. I got a water. We casually chatted while I looked at the menu. She did too, but pretty sure she already knew what she wanted, lol. So, we hung out and ate. I was so wrapped up in chatting. I don't remember what I ordered. Probably nachos, love nachos. Turns out so does she!! Yessssss!!! We finish up and agree it's hot as shit and we have time to kill, so let's head back to her place.

Holy fuck. Okay. Don't panic. Just gonna' go there. Kill some time before that zoo thing we were doing. Fuck. What the hell was it called? Don't matter just breathe so far this is going well minus the whole thumbs up thing you dummy.

Okay back into the car. Wonder if shed let me drive?

Let's not push it.

So, we get back to her place and head back inside. Her son was eating in the living room, and she told him we were taking over the living room. He seemed a little annoyed by it, but listened and grabbed his things and head to his room, I think. We sat down. She asked what I wanted to watch, and I said it didn't matter. I think we put on, like, some movie or something and chatted a little. Then she asked if I ever saw New Girl. Of course I haven't lol. I don't watch *nothing* but I said no and she basically couldn't believe I was human cause it's like the best ever, and so on it went. We chilled, and watched, and chatted. We both multiple times contemplated not going on our planned zoo date. It was hot a fuck and muggy as shit. For real it was gross. But we ultimately decide to go.

Soooo, back to the car we went.

Please ask if I wanna' drive.

Nope she didn't, lol. Back in the passenger seat I go.

~Part II of Our Date~

We head on over to the zoo and along the way I had the bright idea to show her how easy going and fun loving I am. So, what did I do?

Of course, I strike up a conversation with people at a dairy queen we were by at a red light. 'Cause that's normal and she will think it's funny and *not* fear for her life in any way 'cause she's in the car with a crazy person. What can I say. I make smart decisions. So obviously after winning her over, I could tell by the sheer embarrassment on her face followed by the millionth '*I can't believe you just did that, omg*' we finally arrived near the zoo and found a place to park.

Forgot to mention. I'm fat and it's like the sun outside but with wetness. It was gross. But gotta' play it cool cause this is going well and I'd like to not fuck this all up! So, I go to hold her hand and we start to walk. That didn't last long. Hands were sweaty. It was hot and gross out lol.

So, into the zoo we go. It's some light thingy and it was evening so it was actually pretty cool. All different kinds of animals and such made of lights and stuff. Was cool. So, I'm walking around, sweaty and gross, and just enjoying time with this incredible woman. We are chatting and looking at everything. She's taking pics. It's a good time. Although she wore sandals and like regretted it before we even made it in, but we chugged on. Her sore feet and my swamp-ass-having self. I hate walking but I didn't even care because it was so much fun doing it with her. We ended up stopping at one point near some fish lights.

I love fish. Idk if she did but that's where we stopped. Took a couple pics together and I said 'fuck it. Let's go for it and hope for the best.' And I did. I went in for a quick kiss. And it was reciprocated!!

Hell yeah, jimmy boy!!!! You weren't misreading the vibes!!!

We continued on and ended up pausing in front of the eagle's pen. Pen? Cage? House? Idk but the eagle was in there, all bad-ass and looking like freedom and 'murica. I pulled her in for a more intimate kiss. Not too long, 'cause public. Idk how she is about public. *Psssst. Spoiler. Not big on it.* But, I digress. We shared an amazing moment together topped of by, 'wanna' go home? Yes? Awesome cause its gross as fuck out.' And so back we went. Hand in hand. For a little. A short drive later we were back at her place.

~Part Tres of our date~

We head back in and back to the living room.

Was time for more New Girl!! But this time, it was even better. We had an amazing time out and the chemistry was feeling strong. We sat down but this time snuggled up together. It was. Aghhhhhh. She seemed to just snuggle up perfectly against me. I don't remember most of the episodes 'cause I was so focused on playing with her hair and rubbing her arm and back. It was just amazing. Stayed way later than either of us planned because we didn't want it to end. We enjoyed some kisses while we were snuggled up, and let me tell you… Trying to conceal the excitement being made obvious from certain things waking *all the way up*, that was a struggle.

It was amazing. It was our first time meeting. It had been maybe like, 5 or 6 hours by this point, but it had felt like it was just another night after years together. Just felt so natural being there. With her. Cuddled up. Enjoying some kissed and snuggles. I didn't want it to end. Pretty sure we said 'Okay seriously, last episode' like 4 episodes in a row. But, alas, she had work in the morning and I had to get back to work in the morning too, so we had to wrap it up.

So, we got up and I got my things together and we headed outside. Well. Most my things at least. I made sure I left my hat on the couch. It was the first time I had worn it, it's a limited edition I paid too much money for. But, I knew there was no way I wouldn't see her again. High five for stealing a trick I learned from women. Guys can do it too!! But back to that moment. I had my things on to ride home. We hugged and kissed a little more outside. May have been a slight hair pull and an ass grab but I'm a gentleman and would never confirm or deny. We had one last kiss before I headed home. The whole ride I was just captivated by the amazingness that was the past few hours and how I already couldn't wait to see her again.

It's crazy how it's been over a year now and that hasn't changed.

Not wanting any moment with you to end, counting down the minutes till I get to see you again. It's been a wild ride for sure. We have had a lot of ups and downs and have gone through more than I feel most couples do in the beginning, yet I wouldn't change a thing. The feeling of your love is something that I cannot describe with words because I don't think there's words to describe just how pure and warm and amazing it is.

You've stuck by my side through some of the heaviest and ugliest times of my life.

You've seen the darkest parts of me that I've spent so much time burying.

Yet through all that, you loved me harder.

You showed me I'm not alone.

You've shown me what a true partner is.

You've shown me the type of love and compassion I deserve.

You've shown me that it's okay to be taken care of.

It's okay to let someone in.

You've shown me that it's okay to be loved the way I love.

You've truly helped to heal the parts of me you never broke.

I don't know how I got so lucky.

The way all our kids have felt, as if we were all family so quickly, has only gotten stronger. Listening to you talk to my kids while they are away just melts my heart. To hear them talk about how much they love you is the sweetest sound. That day at Darien Lake when they were talking about how they want you as their step mom and can't wait for Jake and Jessa to be their brother and sister was just, beautiful. They joy in Vinny's voice when he tells me about the cat pictures you send him, and how happy it makes him...

I know I couldn't have found a better partner to build a life with.

After all this time I still don't know how I got so lucky. The memories we have made are ones I hope never fade away. We have such an amazing life ahead of us. So many amazing moments waiting to happen. I cannot wait to watch all our kids grow up together. I cannot wait to look out across our yard and see you Winnie the Poohing it while you're in the garden. I still don't know how I got so lucky to be the one that gets to be by your side as all your dreams come true. Knowing how bright the future is because I'll get to enjoy your beautiful smile every day for the rest of my life puts the biggest smile on my face.

I love you so so so much, Gizmo.

There's no one I'd rather do life with, and I'm so thankful I don't need to.

I don't like heights so of course lets get a room so I can look down at the roofs of buildings.

Yeah shes flaming hot.

I know.

Also, so will the hell I'll be in for using this pic!

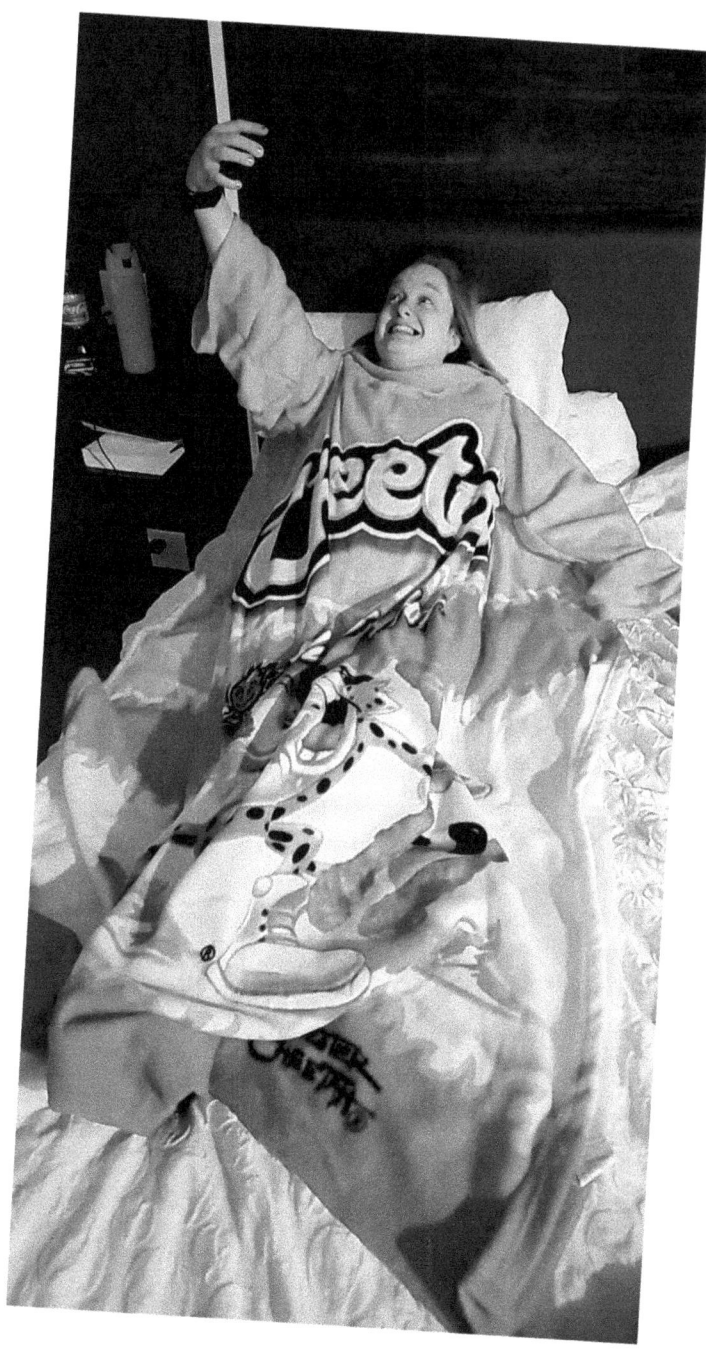

ONE WILD RIDE

Almost a year later we return to where it all started, but this time we aren't alone!

I feel this sums things up well.

Me- "I love you lets be cute."

Her - "Nahhhhhhh."

Someone must have farted.

Also WTF is going on with my hair?

Is this is what hom is?
I love me some hom.

Holy crap a normal cute pic? How the hell did that get in here? Ughhhhh. Shes so damn cute.

I bought a whole ass suit for this.
Her Daughters sweet 16 party.
Was alot of fun

Our first night at Alisons by the fire. LETS GO BUFFALOOOOOOO!

Just a beautiful day at Alisons. Sheesh. Look at how fat i am. Even the filter didn't help

Seeeeeee!

I knew what I was doing. Hell she even rocks it better than I do.

Fucking racing antique cars like a boss ass bitch!

39

WHO THE HELL WROTE THIS THING?

Hey!

My names Jim and in my best The Lonely Island impression, *I WROTE A BOOK MOTHER FUCKER.* I like long walks at the buffet. Doing super random things to hopefully get a laugh which usually doesn't. I drive a truck for a living because of course I do. I grew up in WNY and spent my life wishing I didn't. Why is NYC not its own state yet? Leave the rest of NY alone k thanks. I like getting distracted from what I'm doing by my random thoughts. In my spare time I like to play video games. Build gunpla models. Annoy my beautiful fiancé. Think of fun ways to surprise her.

Like this book for instance.

Surprise babe!! I'm an author now!!!

Acknowledgments

Mathew Ruley for helping make this a reality!!!
Adhd for letting my brain go wild. My motorcycle for getting me to and from this amazing woman. Her Chevy Trax for taking us to and from our lovely date. DoorDash for supplying her kids with food. El Palenque for our delicious food. The Buffalo Zoo for setting the scene for our magical date. The light up fish for the perfect mood lighting for our first kiss! The eagle for being majestic as fuck! New Girl for the being such a snuggle worthy show. And last but not least you for taking this ride with me. Without all of you none of this would be possible.

Thank you!

www.ingramcontent.com/pod-product-compliance
Lightning Source LLC
Chambersburg PA
CBHW051829160426
43209CB00006B/1097